The publishers wish to thank the following
photographers and photographic agencies for their help
in producing this book:

Animals Animals
I. Jeklin: 46
Zig Leszczynski: Back cover, top right, *and* 29, left
Leonard Lee Rue III: 52, top

Ardea (London) Ltd.
J. A. Bailey: 39, bottom
Ian Beames: 45, top
Tony Beamish: front cover
Hans and Judy Beste: 30; 48; 49
Kevin Carlson: 45, bottom
M. D. England: 41
Peter Steyn: 44
Wardene Weisser: 40

Barnaby's Picture Library
B. Stocks: 16, bottom
and 29, right; 31, top left; 37, top; 39, top; 42, bottom;
47; 52, bottom

Liz and Tony Bomford
Back cover, bottom right, and 17, bottom

Bruce Coleman Ltd.
Helmut Albrecht: 55
Jane Burton: Back cover, top left, and 24/25, spread;
5; 54; 58/59, spread

Dian Fossey: 56, top
Dennis Green: 32
Hugo A. Lambrechts: 42, top
Norman Myers: 57
Goetz D. Plage: 50
Allan Power: 21
Mike Price: 9; 56, bottom
Hans Rheinhard: Leading and trailing endpapers; 22,
top; 26; 53, bottom; 58/59, inset
James Simon: 53, middle
Norman Owen Tomalin: 31, bottom
Peter Ward: 33, bottom
Joseph van Wormer: 53, top

David Hosking: 43

Eric Hosking: 27; 31, top right; 33, top; 35; 36; 38

Oxford Scientific Films Ltd.
M. J. Coe: 16, top; 37, bottom
Dr. J. A. L. Cooke: 15; 17, top; 18
and back cover, bottom left; 6; 10; 11, top and bottom;
12; 13, main picture and inset; 14, top and bottom;
19, top, middle and bottom; 20, main picture and inset;
22, bottom; 23; 24/25, inset; 28; 33, middle; 34; 60; 61

Picturepoint Ltd.: 51

First published 1979 by J. M. Dent and Sons Limited,
Aldine House, Welbeck Street, London
Designed and produced for J. M. Dent and Sons Limited by
Asset Publishing Limited
Copyright © 1979 Asset Publishing Limited
All rights reserved
ISBN 0 460 06899 7   Printed in Great Britain

British Library Cataloguing in Publication Data

Builders.—(Animal specialists).
  1. Animals, Habitations of—Juvenile literature
  I. Ellis, Malcolm   II. Series
591.5'6   QL756

ISBN 0-460-06899-7

BUILDERS

Editor: Malcolm Ellis

J. M. Dent and Sons Limited
London · Toronto · Melbourne

Contents

Introduction	8
The Industrious Invertebrates	11
Underwater Builders	21
The Excavators	27
Feathered Architects	35
Mammals as Builders	51

Introduction

Many animals need to build some sort of home for just the same reasons as people do: shelter, warmth and privacy. These structures may be permanent homes, like, for example, the sets of badgers, or temporary arrangements built for the rearing of a family, like the nests of many bird species. Other creatures—notably bees and spiders—combine a shelter with a trap or larder.

Most animals other than birds build 'downwards', that is they burrow or excavate into the ground or into wood. Most of this book is devoted to animals that make a construction above ground level.

Birds, as their many and varied nests testify, are often exceptionally talented builders. Some birds, however, do not build at all; a few, such as bee-eaters and some kingfishers, burrow; others take over the disused homes of other animals, and many make use of sundry holes and crevices they find. It is, however, the nest-building birds that most readily come to mind when we consider animal builders.

Birds' nests, which are often very beautifully constructed, become more noticeable in the winter when the leaves that serve as effective camouflage in the breeding season are no longer present. Probably the best examples of animal builders are the various species of weaver bird, some of which build truly gigantic structures: a flock of up to 300 sociable weavers will build one massive apartment block which takes over an entire tree. In this way the birds gain extra safety from predators. Safety from predators is one of the main benefits birds derive from building a nest, and most nests reflect this in their design and siting.

Few birds live in their nests all year round although several species, notably parrots and tits, use them for roosting. Some mammals, on the other hand, use their homes continuously—beavers, badgers, squirrels and rabbits for example—while others build a succession of temporary residences: such mammals include the great apes and many small rodents. It is perhaps surprising that more mammals do not build above ground level, but many have no need of elaborate structures. Birds, however, need a nest in which to hatch their eggs and rear the young until they become independent.

It is in the insect world, however, that we encounter the most awe-inspiring structures, which are often built by thousands of insects all working together. The towering mounds of termites are sometimes taller than a man, and many times higher than the Empire State Building compared to the size of a man. A termite mound is a model of sophistication, incorporating air conditioning, nurseries, food stores and everything needed for self-contained accommodation. The concrete-like outer casing is as strong as a fortress, although some predators, like the aardvark, make a living by ripping it open and eating the termites.

Other fascinating structures to be found in the insect world include the mountains of pine needles and twigs built by wood ants, the combs of honeybees, and the nests of wasps, which are built from paper manufactured by the wasps.

Spiders are very familiar builders, using their silk to construct an enormous variety of webs and traps, from the shimmering veils of gossamer in the meadows at dawn, to the dark cobwebs in forgotten corners of old houses.

This book shows that man is by no means unique in his ability to design and build complex and completely effective structures. Furthermore, unlike most human habitations, which eventually destroy great areas of the countryside simply by virtue of their numbers, the buildings of animals rarely damage—and often enhance—nature.

Opposite: The nest platform of the orang-utan is a temporary affair, used for a few days and then abandoned. In wet weather the orang-utan shelters under a blanket of leaves.

The Industrious Invertebrates

The most numerous creatures in the animal world are the insects. Usually quite small in size, they are found all over the world and sometimes form immense swarms. Although many insects usually come together only to mate, there are some that build intricate homes and live together in highly organized societies. They are called social insects, and there are four kinds —bees, wasps, ants and termites. Their tools for building are their mouth parts and legs. No living animals apart from man and a few other mammals have such organized lives.

Bees and wasps are related to ants. The majority of bees and wasps, however, do not live highly organized social lives. These are called solitary wasps or bees, but they still have certain building skills. They make quite intricate nests and raise their young on the same general principles as the more familiar honeybees. By looking at these insects it is possible to see how the complex life of social bees and wasps has evolved.

In most solitary egg-laying wasp species the female is called a queen. She builds a nest of many chambers or 'cells' and stocks it with insects she has caught. They are not killed, but paralysed with a poison she injects from the sting at the tip of her abdomen. Then she lays an egg in each cell that contains a paralysed insect, so that there is fresh food available for the young wasp when it hatches.

Most wasps are particular about the shape of their nest and about which kind of insect they put in the 'larder' to feed their young. The potter or mason wasp, as her name suggests, builds a 'pot' of clay or mud. She hunts only small caterpillars to stock the larder for her future offspring. Having paralysed the caterpillar she flies to her pot nest, and pushes it inside the neck of the pot. When she has stored enough caterpillars, she lays a single egg, suspended from the top by a thread of silk. After sealing the neck of her pot with more mud she

Left: Bringing mouthfuls of soft clay to the nest, a mud-dauber wasp constructs the tubular cells that will contain her eggs.

Left, below: Layer by papery layer, a new wasp's nest is built up by a queen wasp in spring, to house the season's brood.

departs and begins a new nest.

The mud dauber wasp carries balls of mud in her jaws to the nest site, which is usually on a tree trunk. Here the wasp skilfully moulds the clay into long nest cells. The tunnel-shaped cells are like the pipes of a large organ. Inside each pipe cell she lays a single egg, and with it are stored paralysed spiders she has caught to provide food for the hungry young when they hatch. Unlike most solitary wasps, the mud dauber female gets some help from her mate. He guards the nest while she is hunting.

The gall wasp is a very strange wasp that causes a plant to build a home for her young. This small, usually black, wasp lays her eggs in the tissues of a leaf of an oak tree. This causes the leaf tissues to grow abnormally. The leaf containing the tiny parasitic egg swells to form a ball. This is the familiar oak apple gall, which turns from green to

Opposite: A close-up of a leaf-cutter ant, carrying a section of leaf, shows why its alternative name is 'parasol ant'.

yellowish-brown with age. When the egg hatches, the larva (young) feeds on the tissues within the gall, until it is large enough to cut a round hole to the outside of the gall and fly off.

The social wasps are like the social bees, building communal nests. There are different kinds of wasp to do different jobs, as in a bee society. There are queens, who are fertile females whose job it is to produce eggs. Workers are also female, but they are unable to produce eggs. The male wasps are the third kind, and their sole job is to mate with any queen whose eggs must be fertilized.

The social wasps' building material consists of wood fibre. This is scraped away from wooden objects, such as posts and rotting tree trunks, with their powerful mandibles or jaws. The fibre is mixed with saliva and worked to a pulp by a worker. The industrious insect draws the pulp out between the two edges of its mandibles, to form a thin strip of paper like a ribbon. The strips are built up into paper combs until a nest is formed. The combs are usually protected by two or three outer 'paper' covers. This gives the wasp's nest a familiar round shape when it is built hanging on a paper stalk from a tree branch.

The comb consists of a single layer of cells, with their openings facing downwards. At any one time this fragile nest may contain eggs and larvae (grubs) at different stages. Pupae are also there, hidden beneath white silken cappings. Although adult wasps feed on nectar and sweet juices such as those from very ripe or rotting fruit, the young must have meat such as flies and caterpillars.

Some solitary bees live similar lives to the solitary wasps. There is a mason bee which, like the mason wasp, builds cells of clay. Sometimes it uses sand as its building material, mixed with its saliva. The European black mason bee usually builds several cells on the side of a large pebble, and then covers them with a finer cement to protect the delicate grubs inside from extremes of heat and cold.

The leaf-cutter bee bores long tunnels in old and rotten wood and lines them with cells made from tightly overlapping pieces of leaf, cut from roses and other plants. The cells are shaped like small thimbles and each one is packed with pollen, a food store for the larvae. Each thimble has an egg laid within and then it is sealed with another piece of leaf, cut to fit the circular hole exactly.

Honeybees and bumblebees are social. Their colonies contain three types of bee—one queen, a few males, called drones, and many workers. The building material of social bees is wax, which they make themselves. It is produced in glands inside the insect's body and released from the underside of the abdomen. The bees mould the wax with their mouth parts and legs.

The bee's amazing skill in architecture is in building the cells of wax. Each cell is hexagonal—that is, it has six sides. The cells are built up in layers to form the familiar honeycomb. What is remarkable is that the hexagon shape is the best shape possible to ensure the most storage space for the least work. A triangular or square cell, built from the same amount of wax, will not hold as much honey as a hexagonal cell. Also, the honeycomb shape of interlocking hexagons is an extremely strong one. Why and how the bee came to choose this shape is baffling and as yet no scientist has been able to give a satisfactory explanation.

The worker bees also make two sizes of wax cells. The smaller ones are used to produce worker bees and also for storing pollen. The larger cells are

Left: A group of nocturnal wasps hang on their nest on a tree in Trinidad. Like many other wasps, they have a painful sting.

Opposite: Worker honey bees move over the wax cells of the comb feeding the tiny curled larvae. After about a week the larvae develop into pupae (inset) from which will emerge the adult bees.

Left: A soldier ant stands guard as busy leaf-cutter ants scurry back to the nest with pieces of leaf for their 'fungus garden'.

Below: Weaver ants use their own larvae as living silk-shuttles, squeezing them to make them produce silk to bind the leaf edges together.

14

used to produce drones and to store honey.

The building skills and social organization of bees and wasps are remarkable, yet they take second place to those of ants. These insects have a much more complex social system. In their buildings they have gardens, nurseries, and even 'farms' where they can keep creatures such as greenflies which they 'milk' like cows. All the 6,000 or more different species of ant are social. Although there are the three basic classes or 'castes' of queen, drone and worker, there are often several forms of the worker caste. Most ants build their nest beneath the ground. Within the nest are several chambers. In one the queen spends her time laying eggs, being groomed, fed and cared for by a number of workers. Her eggs are taken off to other chambers for hatching. Then the young larvae are transported to a nursery for their development. Other chambers are used to store food for the inmates, and usually there is a chamber that is the rubbish dump of the colony.

Of the many kinds of ant, weaver ants are very interesting as builders. In the tropical rain forests of South-East Asia these ants work together to join leaves with silken threads to make a nest in a tree. Several worker ants pull the edges of leaves together. The silk thread is produced by the ants' grub-like larvae. Certain worker ants squeeze the larvae gently in their jaws, and press the mouths of the larvae against the leaf edges. This makes the larvae produce silk. The workers pass the larvae to and fro between the leaf edges in such a way that a web of silk is spun to tie the leaves together. The larvae are used like the shuttle of a loom, or a tube of glue.

In the past many ant species have been credited as active farmers, growing, cultivating and harvesting crops. Today it has been shown that the majority are just harvester ants collecting crops for use in the nest. The leaf-cutter ants are such insects. With their jaws they will snip away at a leaf until a large piece is cut out. Then they hold it aloft and march back to the nest. Because they look as if they are carrying an umbrella, these ants are sometimes called parasol ants. It used to be thought that the ants ate the leaves; but it is known now that they use the leaves to feed a special type of fungus. Then they eat the peculiar small bodies produced by the fungus.

The pastoral ants search for a sweet secretion known as honeydew. Greenflies, scale insects, plant lice and some caterpillars of butterflies produce it as a by-product of their feeding. Some ants tend the greenflies and make them exude the honeydew by stroking them with their antennae. The ants will even drive away intruders with sprays of formic acid. Some ants build shelters on the plant stems to protect the greenfly as they feed.

Termites are often called white ants, but in fact are not very closely related to ants. Termites build their nest, called a termitarium or colony, in the

Below: The bull's horn acacia tree produces special thorns which are hollowed out and used as ant nests. In return the ants will attack animals feeding on the tree.

hollow wood on which they feed. There is a great variety of shapes among termite nests. The nests usually have some sort of ventilating system that regulates the oxygen supply and the temperature of the colony.

One species of termite that lives in West Africa builds a huge nest that is covered by an insulating layer. The centre of the nest contains fungus gardens, which the termites tend and care for so that they can eat the fungi. The gardens receive fresh air by way of channels from a cellar cavity. The stale air is conducted away from the centre to surface exit holes by means of other channels.

A remarkable termite builder is the compass termite. It lives only within 80 km of Darwin in the Northern Territory of Australia. This termite's nest is up to 4 m high and a little less in length. It is wedge-shaped, about a metre wide at ground level and tapering to a thin, serrated top. One face of the nest is slightly convex while the other is vertical.

The reason why this creature is called the compass termite can be understood if the position of the nest is studied. All the mounds stand with the long axis accurately orientated to the north and south. It is thought that the termitarium is built this way to avoid rapid changes of temperature inside the nest. As the sun rises in the east each morning, the east side of the nest will receive its rays. As the sun climbs higher and the strength of its rays increases, the rays will strike more obliquely, until at noon they do not hit the sides of the nest at all. The rays then shine on the other side until the sun sets in the west. Within the nest the termites can move to warmer or cooler places. In cool weather they usually go to the side that is receiving the sun's rays, while if it is quite hot they will move to the shady side.

Spiders are not really insects, but are related to scorpions, mites and ticks. A spider has four pairs of legs while an insect has three pairs; and a spider has only two body parts while an insect has three parts. All the 26,000 or so different species of spider

are able to spin silk, and this is their building material. Silk is spun through the six spinnerets at the tip of the abdomen. The silk is used to enclose the eggs, but it is most famous as the material for intricate and varied webs.

The web functions not merely as a home for the spider, but as a trap for catching prey. There are all shapes and sizes of webs, from triangles and circles to funnels and sheets. Each web-spinning spider can usually be identified by the kind of web it spins. The silk of spiders is a protein, and is produced as a liquid. The silk does not harden as a result of drying in the air, but from the actual drawing out process as it leaves the spinnerets. It is extremely strong and elastic. The webs of some spiders are so strong that they are used by the people of some tropical countries, such as New Guinea, as nets for catching fish.

A spider is always safely attached to its web by a line of dry silk. This drag-

Opposite, top: Several termites make foraging tunnels in a pile of elephant dung.

Opposite, bottom: Like the remains of a burnt-out forest, hundreds of termite mounds are scattered starkly over the landscape.

Above: A spider's silk is one of the strongest and most versatile of building materials. This deadly poisonous black widow spider is guarding silken cocoons that contain her eggs.

Left: No less lovely for being familiar, a spider's silken cobweb sparkles with dew.

17

line can be compared to the safety line used by mountaineers. If a spider is brushed off some object, it is quite common to see it swaying in mid-air suspended by its life-saving dragline.

The dragline is also important as it suggests a possible explanation of how spiders first began to make webs. Quite early in the history of spiders, those that had silk draglines probably had a particular spot they used as a home base or hiding place. The approaches to it must soon have become coated with threads of silk, and the spider no doubt learnt that trembling of the threads meant an insect was passing over them. This kind of primitive web can be seen in some living spiders. The round, bluish-looking webs that are found in the corners of windows are primitive webs. The next stage in web development was making the 'mat' much bigger so that there was a better chance of catching prey. The 'cobwebs' in the corners of rooms illustrate this type.

Then certain spiders built their living quarters by the main web, in the form of a silken tube. The web is usually like a hammock. The tiny money spiders construct this kind of web, but they do not have a silken tube in which to wait. They hang themselves upside down under the sheet or hammock waiting for an insect to be caught.

Below: A spider waits in its web for prey.

The most intricate webs of all are made by the orb web spiders. This family includes the common garden spider, also known as the cross or diadem spider. The web of all orb web spiders is a round structure, sometimes reaching a very large size. The tropical orb spiders spin webs with a diameter of 2.5 m.

Most web-building spiders have very poor eyesight, but their sense of touch is very sensitive. If the prey stops moving when caught in the orb web of the garden spider, the spider goes into the middle of its web and plucks the lines radiating out from the middle. Eventually it detects the prey by the dampened vibrations of the plucked line. It quickly identifies the prey by touch. If it is a butterfly or moth, the spider rapidly enshrouds it in a mist of silk. This is because quite often butterflies and moths are strong enough to escape, leaving masses of scales stuck to the web's threads. Other insects are bitten and injected with poison to immobilize them.

The trapdoor spiders of tropical and subtropical countries are related to the large, hairy, bird-eating spiders of South America. They do not build webs, but live in specially constructed retreats in the ground. Trapdoor spiders dig a shaft in the ground which may be up to 30 cm deep and 2 cm in diameter. The walls of the shaft are prevented from caving in by silk, which is spun around the soil particles. The shaft is then lined with a continuous tube of fine silk. The shaft is completed with a well-fitted trapdoor, made from layers of silk and soil. The trapdoor has two gripping points on the underside that the spider can grip with its feet, so no would-be intruder can gain entry.

Most trapdoor spiders use their hole as a spying base. When prey comes near enough, the spider, which has been peeping through a crack in the slightly raised lid, springs the lid up, rushes out, pounces on its prey and puts its fangs into it. Then it drags the paralysed victim back into its tube, pulling the trapdoor firmly down behind it.

Top: Carefully a garden spider carries its caddis fly prey, neatly trussed in silk, to a safe place where it can be eaten at leisure.

Middle: Part of the silk-lined burrow of a trapdoor spider has been cut away to show the spider at the bottom.

Bottom: Ready to pounce, the trapdoor spider lifts the lid on top of its tube trap.

Underwater Builders

The most accomplished builders of the marine world are without doubt the corals. Coral is actually composed of millions of tiny marine animals called polyps, which are closely related to sea anemones. In fact they look so alike that a coral polyp could be described as an anemone that has taken to making a hard skeleton of limestone (calcium carbonate). Each polyp varies from a few millimetres to about 2.5 cm in length. Although some corals live a solitary life, most live together, not just in hundreds, but in thousands of millions. In shallow, warm, tropical waters around the world certain kinds of corals have built up the great coral reefs. It takes a long time—thousands upon thousands of years—for a large coral reef to form. Each coral polyp, with its chalky, hard skeleton around itself, is attached to the skeletons of other corals. The tiny, tentacled heads stick out at the surface and filter food from the water. As the founders of a colony die, later generations of polyps build up on the hard limestone skeletons.

The most famous coral reef is the Great Barrier Reef that runs down the eastern coast of Australia for 2,100 km. Some corals grow in strange shapes, and their common names give some idea of their form. For example, a few of the common corals are staghorn, organ pipe, brain, finger, knobbed, and lettuce corals.

The seas of the world contain many varied fish, the majority of which show little instinct for building a home for themselves or a nest for their offspring. Shoaling fish, such as cod, herring and haddock, gather together in the breeding season. They release their millions of eggs or sperm into the water, letting chance be the main factor in fertilization. However, a few fish show more parental care during the breeding season, and may even build nests for the eggs and future young.

The small gobies found throughout the seas of the world become attentive parents during the breeding season. A mated pair will clean a rock or piece of coral, or find an empty shell, so that the female can lay her eggs there. The male guards her and the 'nest', and when she departs, after laying a clutch of about 100 eggs, he becomes a model father. He oxygenates the eggs by fanning them with his tail and watches over them until they hatch after about two weeks. Many gobies also dig holes in the sand or mud in which to live.

Some species of the brilliantly coloured wrasse make more elaborate nests of seaweed and other marine weed. Both male and female help to wedge the nest in a rock crevice. In the middle of the tangled mass the eggs are laid, but as yet no adult has been seen to show any further care. Others, such as the cuckoo wrasse, dig a nest in sand using the body and tail. The male makes the nest, then entices a female to join him.

The jawfish are so called because of their huge mouths. They dig burrows 30 to 35 cm in length—three times the length of the fish. There is an enlarged internal chamber which is lined with bits of coral and rock. At the entrance to its home the jawfish often builds up a small crater. Perhaps this provides better protection. When danger threatens, the jawfish dives inside the burrow, tail first.

It is among the freshwater fish that excellent nest builders and caring parents are found. The common bullhead or horned pout is an extremely protective parent. In a specially constructed hole, or sometimes in a water

Opposite: In warm tropical waters corals form strange and often brilliantly coloured shapes, building up over the centuries to become huge coral reefs. The skeletons of some kinds of gorgonian 'soft' coral (inset) are used to make coral jewellery.

Left: A juvenile clown wrasse, one of the many colourful species of wrasse. Some species make nests of weed, others dig holes in the sandy sea bed.

rat's old tunnel, the female lays a few thousand eggs. For the next week the male guards, cleans and oxygenates the mass of eggs through their incubation period. After they hatch, the male looks after the small jet-black babies until they are 5 cm long.

Some freshwater fish make quite elaborate nests from bubbles, or pieces of water plants. The paradise fish, gouramis and Siamese fighting fish build nests of bubbles. The nest is from 4 to 12 cm in diameter and is dome-shaped, sometimes rising 5 cm above the surface of the water. The bubbles are produced by the male in his mouth, and each contains a small amount of mucus. This prevents them bursting like ordinary soap bubbles. Each male courts a female and excites her to release her eggs beneath the nest. He fertilizes them and places them in the nest, guarding and tending them. The males are also very protective about the territory around the nest, fighting any intruders. This is how the Siamese fighting fish won its name.

Above: The lovely paradise fish is one of several kinds of fish which build bubble nests at the water surface.

Left: In ponds and streams, caddis fly larvae build themselves protective shells of small stones, shells or weed fragments, which also act as camouflage.

The male of various kinds of stickleback builds a very fine nest from aquatic plants among the weeds, at the beginning of the breeding season. The plants are stuck together with a sticky secretion from his kidneys. The stickleback even shapes the nest by rubbing himself against the material. When completed, his nest has a neat tunnel in it which allows clean water to pass through.

The male then attempts to court a female that is full of eggs. He coaxes her with a zig-zag dance until she enters his nest and lays some eggs. Impolitely she is then chased away, her job done, although a succession of brides will follow until the nest is full of eggs. The male guards the nest until the fry hatch and grow old enough to fend for themselves.

The only spider in the world to live permanently underwater is the water spider of freshwater streams. To do this it constructs for itself a diving air bell, a thimble-shaped bell of silk. The bell is made by spinning a platform of silk between the stems of water plants, with strands of silk running out to other vegetation as holding lines. Air is then released beneath the platform and it bulges upwards until it is the shape of a thimble.

The air is a breathing supply for the spider, as it is unable to use the oxygen dissolved in the water. To obtain the air for its bell the spider rises to the surface of the water. Then, hanging head down in the water, it pushes the tip of its abdomen up into the air. With a sudden jerk of its abdomen and the hind pair of legs, a bubble of air is trapped beneath the spider. The spider then swings or crawls down water plants to its bell, and releases the air into it. The spider uses the bell as its home, waiting there for prey, such as an aquatic insect or its larva, to pass close by. The spider then dashes out to seize it and returns to the bell to eat it.

In freshwater streams are found numerous larvae of the caddis flies. The adult flies are like brownish moths, with hairs instead of scales on their wings.

The larvae live in water and are very curious creatures. When the eggs hatch in the water, a larva begins to spin a tube of silk. The completed tube, open at one end, protects the larva's soft body and gills. Each species of caddis larva has its own method of decorating its tube. The great red sedge caddis fly larva cuts leaves into small fragments, and these are stuck on to the tube to give it a regular pattern. The Welshman's button caddis fly larva uses sand grains, while the silverhorn caddis fly larva uses twigs, stones and leaf fragments. The various materials are stuck to the tube with the larva's silk.

The behaviour of sticking materials to its tube has given the caddis larva its name. A 'caddis man' is an old name for a pedlar who wandered the countryside with his clothes decorated with samples of his wares.

Most caddis fly larvae push their head and legs out of the open ends of their tube to feed on leaves and stems of water plants. One species, however, makes a trumpet-shaped silk net facing upstream from the open end of its tube. This traps any tiny animals or plants carried by the current, which are then eaten by the larva.

Below: A male dwarf gourami excitedly urges his bride towards the nest he has built to contain and protect their eggs.

Right: In flamboyant splendour a Siamese fighting fish spreads his fins to attract a female to his bubble nest.

Inset: The water spider is able to live underwater by constructing a silk globe which it fills with air, and uses as a diving bell in which to draw breath.

The Excavators

Many animals construct their homes by digging tunnels and dens underground. Where several animals of the same species live together, they often excavate a highly complicated system of tunnels, sleeping chambers and entrance or exit holes. The excavators include a great variety of creatures, each digging a different kind of underground home.

The aardvark is a shy, nocturnal animal of the African grasslands. Pig-like in appearance, it has pinkish-brown, bristly skin, big ears and a long snout. It eats termites and ants, which it scoops up with its very long and sticky tongue.

A solitary animal, the aardvark spends the daytime in its burrow. The burrow is usually about 4 m long, with a chamber at the far end. No nest or bed is made. The aardvark excavates with its forefeet, which are very powerful and equipped with four strong claws; it kicks the soil backwards with its hindfeet, which have five claws. As it digs, it folds back its long ears and shuts its nostrils, to keep soil out. Some farmers regard the aardvark as a nuisance because it burrows under fences, and because domestic animals sometimes fall down aardvark burrows and are injured. Abandoned aardvark burrows are often used by warthogs or spotted hyenas.

A well-known animal excavator is the badger. This nocturnal mammal is a relative of the stoat and weasel. It has a powerful, stocky body with short, sturdy legs and strong claws. Found throughout the British Isles and much of Europe and Asia, the badger usually lives in woodland—particularly where it borders pasture—and in hedgerows, on cliffs and in quarries.

The underground home of the badger is called a set, and is generally excavated in a woodland hillside with adequate undergrowth to provide cover. The set may extend 3 to 6 m below the surface, and consists of several tunnels and chambers, often at more than one level. There is usually more than one opening to the set. The main entrance is partly hidden by a mound of earth turned out when the set was excavated.

Outside the breeding season, several badgers usually share a home. They keep the set extremely clean. Nearby, the badger digs small pits for its droppings. It regularly changes its bedding, collecting a fresh supply of bracken, dry leaves or grass. Old bedding is thrown out and left near the main entrance to the set. Trees near the set are used by the badgers as scratching posts to clean and sharpen their front claws.

During the spring breeding season, male and female badgers the boar and sow, pair up and make their own home. The sow prepares a special chamber, which she lines with moss and grass, where she gives birth to her young.

Unlike most animals that excavate their homes, the rabbit is not especially adapted for digging. Nevertheless, it constructs a large and complex system of burrows called a warren. Warrens are found in all sorts of places: farmland, sand dunes, marshes, moorland and cliffs.

The rabbit uses its forepaws to loosen the soil, which is kicked back-

Above: The odd-looking aardvark, an inhabitant of African savannahs, uses its powerful forelimbs to excavate deep burrows where it usually rests by day.

Opposite: Although it is a well-known animal, the badger is not often seen, since it only emerges from its burrow, or 'set', at dusk.

wards by the hindfeet. Stones that cannot be dislodged by paws are removed by teeth. The tunnels are about 15 cm in diameter, sometimes widening to about 30 cm to make 'passing places'.

The warren consists of many tunnels leading to several chambers, and bolt-runs leading to emergency exits. Warrens vary in size and may be extensive when occupied by a large rabbit colony; sometimes the topsoil is disturbed, resulting in damage to field boundaries and hedges.

An adult rabbit, or buck, does not make itself a bed but sleeps on the bare earth. The female rabbit, or doe, digs a burrow, called a 'stop', for her young. This is lined with hay or straw, and fur removed from her underparts. The stop may be added on to the main warren or excavated as a separate burrow, which may eventually become a new warren.

Several members of the rodent family excavate homes, one of the best known being the prairie dog of North America. Prairie dogs live in large colonies, and their extensive underground burrows, which cover several square kilometres, are known as 'dog towns'.

The main tunnel descends steeply for about 2 m, then turns slightly upwards. About a metre below the entrance hole is a chamber where a prairie dog can sit and listen for danger, such as a predator, on the surface. The upward turn in the tunnel causes an air pocket to be made and helps protect the burrow from flooding.

The main tunnel may be as long as 30 m, with chambers and passages leading from it. At the far end the nursery chamber is lined with soft grasses. As another precaution against flooding, the entrance hole is raised by a mound of earth. The prairie dogs nibble away any vegetation within several metres of the entrance hole, which gives them a clear view of the surroundings—and any predators.

Below: A rabbit's-eye view of another rabbit, about to enter one of the holes in the warren. Rabbits are such keen diggers that the name warren is now used to describe any area riddled with passages.

Closely related to prairie dogs are the eight species of marmot, which have largely been eradicated from lowland areas and are now confined to the mountains of North America, Europe and Asia. They dig burrows up to 3 m underground.

The common hamster is a solitary nocturnal rodent of Europe and Asia, inhabiting plains, cultivated land and riverbanks. It has broad feet with strong claws. The hamster digs a number of tunnels, measuring about 6 to 8 cm in diameter, with several chambers for its nest and food stores. The hamster hibernates in the winter and has been found as far as 2 m underground.

The curious duck-billed platypus of eastern Australia and Tasmania is another animal that excavates. Living in rivers, streams and lakes, it digs a burrow up to 12 m long in a bank. Long tunnels are made only by the female and used as nesting places; shorter tunnels are made by both sexes.

The duck-billed platypus digs with the powerful claws on its webbed front feet, and also uses its beak-like muzzle. The excavated soil is not thrown out but pressed down on the floor and flattened by the platypus's tail, resulting in an arch over a level floor.

The female makes her nest from wet vegetation, which she carries between her belly and forward-tucked tail. The duck-billed platypus is a monotreme, a very primitive marsupial or egg-laying mammal, and the nest of wet material probably helps maintain a damp atmosphere in the burrow so that the eggs do not dry up.

An excavator that lives almost continuously underground is the mole. The mole has short, shovel-shaped front legs that turn outwards, and it digs with a breast-stroke type of action. When a mole is tunnelling just below the ground, the displaced soil forms ridges on the surface. When excavating deeper tunnels, 5 to 20 cm underground, the mole pushes the loosened soil forwards and, at intervals, upwards, to form molehills.

The mole's nest is lined with grass, moss and dead leaves, and is used for sleeping and breeding. Above the nest is an extra large molehill called a fortress. A maze of tunnels generally surrounds the nest. The mole tunnels to find food, such as earthworms, slugs and insect larvae. It sometimes makes long surface tunnels in search of a mate in spring; otherwise it leads a solitary life.

One of the largest excavations is made by the polar bear. The female polar bear spends the whole winter in a den, where the cubs are born and

Below: A prairie dog on the look-out at his particular patch of 'dog town'. Although hundreds of prairie dogs may colonize an area, each family has its own small territory.

Bottom, right: Built for a life of digging, a mole surfaces briefly before turning its huge forepaws downwards again to tunnel rapidly through the earth.

nursed until spring. The mother bear may fast for as long as 140 days as she suckles her cubs, living on the body fat built up during the summer.

The den is excavated in the autumn, usually in a snowdrift on the leeward side of a hill. A 2 m tunnel leads to an oval chamber about 2 to 3 m wide and 1 m high. The pregnant female bear retires to the den in October or November and her cubs are born in December or January. The entrance hole is sealed by winter snow and the mother bear's body heat keeps the den about 22°C warmer than the air outside. This heat also keeps open the air vent made by the bear.

After birth, the cubs are kept warm by the mother's thick fur and grow rapidly on her rich milk. In March or April the female bear digs through the winter layer of snow covering the entrance hole and emerges with her cubs. In very cold weather, male polar bears and females without cubs make dens to shelter in for short periods.

Mammals are not the only animals to excavate; several species of bird also dig holes when making their nests. The woodpeckers number more than 200 species, and are found in most countries. They can be recognized by the drumming sounds they make as they peck rapidly into the trunks of trees with their long, powerful, chisel-shaped beaks. They are searching for insects under the bark, or excavating holes for nesting. A rotten tree is often chosen for the nesting site, though woodpeckers have even been known to use telegraph poles. The nest hole is partly filled with wood chippings, on which the woodpecker lays its eggs.

Two species of woodpecker that live in the deserts of the south-western USA excavate their nest holes in the giant saguaro cacti, which grow 10 to 16 m tall. A tunnel about 20 cm long leads to a cool chamber lined with cactus sap.

Barbets are plump, sturdy-billed birds of tropical forests. In South America, the black-spotted barbet excavates a nest hole up to a height of 6 m in a tree; it also uses abandoned woodpecker holes. The coppersmith barbet of oriental forests tunnels about 40 cm into the rotten wood of a tree trunk or branch and lays its eggs on the bare wood.

Left: Like most kingfishers, the sacred kingfisher builds a nest hole at the end of a tunnel, in a bank close to the water where it hunts its fish prey.

The nesting site of the common kingfisher of Britain and Europe is usually situated in a riverbank, often a sandy bank beneath overhanging trees. It can often be identified by the white, bird-droppings around the entrance hole. The kingfisher digs a tunnel that slopes upwards for about a metre, ending in a round nesting chamber. Undigested fish bones ejected by the kingfisher dry into a bed of crumbled fragments, on which the eggs are laid.

Several species of motmot live in the tropical forests of Central and South America. The blue-crowned motmot excavates a tunnel up to 2 m long.

Similar in appearance to the motmots are the colourful bee-eaters of the Old World. They live mainly in southern Europe, Africa and Asia. The European bee-eater has nested in Britain. One kind, the rainbow bee-eater or rainbow-bird, occurs in Australia. Most bee-eaters nest in colonies. They make a long tunnel in a bank, often by a river, or sometimes on level ground. The nesting chamber is unlined. The two to five or more eggs are pure white. Both parents take part in ex-

Opposite, top, left: The rapid tapping made by the great spotted woodpecker, as it punches a hole in a tree trunk, is a distinctive woodland sound.

Opposite, top, right: Noisy and gregarious, carmine bee-eaters gather in large colonies to excavate their nest holes in a sandy cliff face.

Opposite, bottom: The female polar bear avoids the worst of the Arctic winter by digging a den deep in the snow, where she gives birth to her cubs.

cavating the tunnel, incubating the eggs, and caring for the young.

Another bird that nests in colonies is the sand martin. A sandy cliff, sand pit or steep riverbank is used as the nesting site. Using its small beak, the sand martin digs a burrow nearly a metre long with a small chamber at the end, which it lines with hay, straw and feathers.

Several species of insect could also be described as excavators. Most wood-boring insects belong to the beetle family. The spruce bark beetle or engraver beetle bores a vertical tunnel into pine or spruce trees by eating its way through the bark. It lays its eggs along the sides of the tunnel. The ambrosia beetle tunnels into the wood of dead or fallen trees, rather than the bark.

Another wood-boring insect is the wood wasp or horntail. The female wood wasp cuts a hole in the wood of a dead tree with her long, saw-like, egg-laying organ, which is called an ovipositor. She then lays her eggs inside the hole.

Some species of wasp dig holes and tunnels in sandy soil to lay their eggs. Many kinds of ant excavate underground nests, digging a maze of tunnels in soil, dead wood or bark.

Above: The sand martin digs a long burrow into a sandy cliff or riverbank, with its nesting chamber at the far end. Dozens of martins may use the same site for their nests (below left), creating a maze of tunnels.

Opposite: A female wood wasp starts to bore a hole in a tree trunk. Inside it she will lay an egg, which will develop into a larva (middle left) that eats into the wood.

33

Feathered Architects

Hornbills are unusual-looking birds, so named because of their enormous, down-curved beaks, which bear a peculiar horny growth known as the casque. This varies in size and shape according to the species of hornbill, and is nearly always smaller and less prominent in the female. Although the casque makes the beak appear almost too heavy for the bird to support, it is actually quite light, as the horny outer shell contains honeycomb-like cellular tissue. Why hornbills have such enormous beaks surmounted by a casque is a mystery.

In common with excavators such as the woodpeckers and barbets, hornbills usually nest in holes in trees. There is, however, one aspect of the hornbills' nesting habits which makes them unique among birds. The hornbills plaster mud around the nest hole opening and gradually reduce its size. The female then enters the hole and, using her own droppings, continues to plaster the opening until all that remains is a tiny hole just big enough for the male hornbill to get the tip of his beak through.

The plaster sets hard and the female is incarcerated within the hole, entirely dependent upon the male to bring food, which he passes through the tiny opening. While safely within the nest the female sheds all her wing and tail feathers and is flightless.

Completely protected from predators, the female lays three to five eggs which hatch after about 30 days, in the case of most of the smaller species of hornbill; or one or two eggs which hatch after about 50 days, in the case of the larger hornbills. Once the eggs hatch, the male has to bring food not only for the female, but also for the nestlings.

After six or seven weeks, when the young are partly grown, the female breaks open the plaster and emerges to help the male with the task of collecting the increasing quantities of insects and other food needed to feed their growing family. Once she has gone, the young hornbills at once seal themselves in again, using their own droppings.

It is quite cramped within the nesthole and the youngsters squat with their tails held up against their backs. They are now strong enough to back up to the opening to defaecate out of it, and throw out food remains with their beaks. When their feathers are grown the young hornbills break out of the nest hole and thereafter accompany their parents, learning to catch insects for themselves. Among some large forest hornbills, which have only one or two young that feed mainly on abundant fruits, the male continues to feed the female and young for the entire fledging period. Some females are known to remain incarcerated within the nest hole for as long as

Opposite: As tiny as its builder, a hummingbird's nest forms a neat cup to enclose the nestlings.

Below: Voluntary imprisonment—the female hornbill is sealed inside a hole in a tree for as long as it takes to hatch and raise her young.

112 days. The African ground hornbills, turkey-sized and largest of all the hornbills, usually nest in a hole in a tree or in a stump, or a crevice among rocks. The hole is lined with a few leaves. Unlike the other hornbills, the female ground hornbills are not walled in.

Rather in the manner of the typical hornbills, some of the nuthatches—small, rather woodpecker-like birds—nest in holes and plaster the opening with mud. However, the nuthatches merely reduce the size of the opening so that it is just big enough to allow them to come and go, but keeps out larger birds. Among the nuthatches which do this is the one that is familiar in many parts of Britain and Europe, and which also occurs in north-west Africa and much of Asia.

It is not too fussy about whether or not it uses nesting material: sometimes it does not bother and simply lays its six to nine white eggs, which are usually spotted with reddish-brown, on the debris at the bottom of the hole. Sometimes it gathers a fairly large collection of material such as dead leaves and pieces of bark, but still does not make a proper nest.

Many other kinds of bird also take advantage of the cement-like qualities of mud as a building material: one of these is the song thrush. This garden bird usually nests in a tree, hedge, bush, ivy or other vegetation growing against a wall, or sometimes even inside a building. The cup-shaped nest is built by the female using material such as grass, roots and leaves, and is frequently lined with mud.

Three species of bird which live in Australia and another in New Guinea, that build cup-shaped nests almost entirely of mud, have come to be known as the mudnest builders. One species, the black and white magpie-lark or mudlark, is one of the best-known Australian birds. It is common throughout Australia wherever there is water but does not breed in Tasmania. It is found in city suburbs, in gardens, along roadsides and in open fields, but especially along the edges of lakes and dams. The magpie-lark

needs to live close to water to have a plentiful supply of mud, and usually chooses to build on a bare horizontal branch or in the fork of a tall waterside tree. The nest, made from mud strengthened with grass, measures approximately 15 cm across, 9 cm deep and 2 cm thick. It takes up to 20 days to complete, and the three or four white eggs with violet and purplish-brown blotches are laid on consecutive days. A constant supply of mud is a controlling factor in the magpie-lark's nesting activities.

Unlike the magpie-lark, where the pair defend a breeding territory, two of the other mudnest builders nest in closely-knit communities. One kind, the apostlebird, is so named because it often goes about in parties of twelve. A community of the white-winged chough (another mudnest builder) may consist of 8 to 20 birds. All members of the community help build the nests, incubate the eggs and feed the young; and if danger threatens, all of them attack or mob the intruder.

The white-winged chough's mud nests are built 10 to 12 m above the ground on the horizontal branches of a tree. Sometimes more than one female lays in the same nest, so a nest may eventually contain as many as nine eggs, although four is the average number. The nest is too small to hold more than four growing nestlings and many come to grief; they sometimes get trampled to death, often as the

Above: The nuthatch, like the hornbill, almost seals off its nest hole with mud, but leaves enough space for the parents to enter and leave.

result of more than one adult wanting to 'mother' them.

Living in the rain forest of West Africa are two strange bird species known as picathartes or bare-headed rockfowl. Despite their name, these birds are quite unfowl-like in appearance and habits: one kind has the bare skin of its head coloured creamy-yellow, with two circular, black 'ear' patches; the other has a red, blue and black head. Both birds are of similar size, measuring about 36 cm in length from beak to tail. Rockfowl seldom fly, but move across the forest floor in a series of hops. These birds construct a cup-like nest of mud, interwoven with vegetation and reinforced around the rim with small sticks, and attach it to a rock face deep in the forest. Often several nests are built close together, invariably below an overhang to protect them from the rain, which would cause them to disintegrate and collapse.

The nests made by flamingos normally consist simply of a mound of mud 15 to 36 cm high, with a shallow depression scooped out of the top by the bird's beak. In the depression a single egg is laid. The flamingo sits incubating on top of the nest mound, with its long legs folded beneath it. The egg takes about 28 days to hatch.

All flamingos nest in colonies, often of enormous size. In East Africa a single colony of more than 900,000 pairs, and a grand total of as many as a million pairs, have been recorded nesting on just one Rift Valley lake.

Also in Africa, as well as in Madagascar and south-western Arabia, lives a small, sombre-brown coloured relation of the herons and storks, called the hammerhead or hammerkop. This bird uses mud to construct its fortress-like nest, which is so strong that it is able to support the weight of a full-grown person standing on the top of it.

The pair of hammerheads usually choose a tree growing close to water and build in a fork from 5 to 20 m or more above the ground. They bring sticks and other vegetation, which is mixed with mud, and may incorporate into the nest an incredible assortment of rubbish such as old rags, bones,

rusty tins, matchboxes and even dead birds and tortoise shells. The hammerhead incubates three to six white eggs.

The entrance to the nest is just big enough to admit the owners and is positioned so that it cannot be reached by predatory snakes and small mammals. Pairs of barn owls, however,

often get in and eject the hammerheads, and sometimes a swarm of bees takes over the nest. Birds of prey, including owls, sometimes nest on the top of an abandoned hammerhead nest. When the hammerhead's nest begins to disintegrate a pair of Egyptian geese may gain admittance and nest inside.

A structure comparable to the hammerhead's is built by a small, thrush-like South American bird called the rufous ovenbird. Its nest, like a domed

Above: A pair of rufous ovenbirds prepare to bring up their young inside their solidly constructed mud nest.

Left: A group of lesser flamingos building up their pot-shaped nests in the shallow waters of a soda lake in Kenya.

mud-oven, is built in the open, often on a fence-post, a bare branch of a tree, or the eaves of a house. The rufous ovenbird builds a new nest each year, but as the old ones are so strong and durable they often remain for several years and are used by other birds, including swallows.

Many members of the swallow family (which includes the martins) are themselves quite accomplished builders. Many make their nests using tiny pellets of mud. Some species build a fairly simple open cup, others an enclosed nest with an entrance hole; some add an entrance tunnel, which leads to the actual nesting chamber. The nests are built in a hole, often in a tree, or on the face of a cliff or building, and sometimes even inside an occupied building. Swallows commonly live and nest near human habitations. Many members of the family are almost entirely dependent upon humans for their nesting places.

Among the most familiar and best-loved of the swallows is the kind which nests in Britain and Europe, and in much of the northern hemisphere. This swallow frequently nests in farm buildings (in America it is called the barn swallow), garages and other outhouses. It seldom settles on the ground, except when collecting mud for nest building. Then numbers of swallows congregate at muddy places, particularly in farmyards, at pools of water along rough farm tracks, and the muddy edges of streams and ponds. The cup-shaped nest is made from tiny pellets of mud, mixed with a little straw, and is usually lined with feathers. It is frequently placed on a beam or stuck against a wall, often utilizing a nail or other projection to provide extra support. Sometimes several pairs of swallows nest close together. Each pair normally lay two clutches, consisting of four to six white eggs, which are speckled with reddish-brown. Occasionally a pair lay a further clutch and succeed in raising three broods of young during a season.

Studies have shown that the same pair of swallows frequently return to the same locality each year to nest—often to the same building, where they sometimes reuse, after renovation, their old nest. Sometimes one of the pair has a new mate, and sometimes both return to the same site, but each with a different partner. Young swallows rarely return to their exact place of birth to breed, although many return to nest close by.

The American cliff swallow also commonly lives and nests in close proximity to human development. It has greatly benefited from the spread of human population across North America: the clearance of vast tracts of land for farming has provided enormous open spaces where the cliff swallow can 'hawk' insects, while it has largely forsaken cliffs in favour of the surfeit of sheltered nest sites provided by man-made structures.

It usually nests in colonies, sometimes of considerable size—one barn in Wisconsin, USA, contained over 2,000 nests — although colonies are normally far smaller. Although the cliff swallow usually nests on buildings,

Below: Tucked under the eaves of a house, this swallow's nest may be renovated for re-use by the migrating swallows year after year.

38

Left: The swift, master of flight, rarely alights on the ground, but will cling to the sides of its nest to feed its young.

often under the eaves, and beneath bridges, some cliff colonies still exist, and more rarely it nests on trees. The nests are gourd-shaped, made from pellets of mud.

Snakes sometimes manage to enter the nests. Cowbirds also get in and parasitize the swallows. The main menace is the house sparrow, which was introduced into North America from Europe. Pairs of house sparrows often take over a nest after the swallows have built it. There is an account of a pair of sparrows which took over a newly-completed nest, but after laying one egg were ejected by the swallows, which then laid their own eggs. The swallows hatched all the eggs together, but the young swallows soon died, leaving the sparrow to be successfully raised by the foster parents.

House martins sometimes nest in quite large colonies. The nests are often built close together, sometimes even overlapping, often beneath bridges spanning rivers, but also beneath motorway bridges, where the birds seem unconcerned by the thousands of vehicles which speed below throughout the day and night. True to its name, the house martin is commonly found around houses, often in cities and suburbs. It usually builds its nest beneath the eaves and is sometimes regarded as a nuisance because of the mess made by its droppings. The house martin also nests on sea and inland cliffs.

Superficially similar in appearance to the swallows and martins, but not closely related to them, are the swifts.

Swifts have long wings and are primarily adapted for sailing through the air in high-speed flight. The typical swifts are the most aerial of all birds; they feed entirely in the air and in many cases even mate and collect their nesting material while on the wing. They glue the material together with saliva, which is produced by their unusually large salivary glands.

Several mainly South-East Asian swifts, which because of their small size are called swiftlets, use little or no 'proper' nesting material, but rely on their saliva; this rapidly dries and hardens on exposure to air. One kind, the edible-nest swiftlet, makes its cup-shaped nest entirely from its own saliva. Its name provides the clue to the fact that it is this bird's translucent 'white' nests which are used to make the famed bird's nest soup. The nests contain very few impurities and are the most highly prized of all nests. Other swiftlets' nests, which contain feathers or vegetable matter and require extensive cleaning, are not so esteemed.

Below: Almost ready to learn to fly, young house martins peep out of their cosy mud nest on a house wall.

Right: With her slender beak, a hummingbird sucks nectar from flowers and then passes it on to feed her nestlings.

Swiftlets' nests have been regarded for centuries as a delicacy by the Chinese and some other Asian people. Although credited with being a tasty, nourishing and even an aphrodisiac food, the nests have little nutritional value. A thriving nest-collecting industry exists, particularly in parts of Borneo and the Philippines. Despite the intensive harvesting of the nests, there appears to be little effect on the overall population of the swiftlets.

The swiftlets nest (often in enormous colonies of well over a million birds) in mountain and coastal caves. They are able to fly and nest deep inside the pitch-dark caves, thanks to a means of navigation similar to that used by most bats: echo-location. The female swiftlet lays two eggs, which both birds incubate for just over three weeks. The young take a remarkably long time to fledge. Before they can find their way out of the caves, sometimes a distance of 500 m or more through the pitch-dark, their echo-location must be fully developed.

The nests made by the crested tree swifts are small, shallow cups made from saliva, mixed with feathers, tiny scraps of bark and lichen or moss. They are attached to the side of a horizontal slender branch, generally one bare of leaves. Seen from below, the nests appear merely as a knot in the wood. Just big enough to hold a single egg, the nests are so fragile that the birds dare not place their full weight on them. They perch across the branch, beside the nest, and cover the egg with the fluffed-out feathers of their belly and vent.

The palm swift of tropical Africa and Asia usually nests on the underside of a hanging, swaying, palm leaf. The nest consists of a hammock-like pad, made mainly from feathers which are glued to the leaf with the palm swift's saliva. There is a small projecting rim to prevent the two eggs from rolling out, and as an added safeguard, the eggs are glued to the nest. Because the leaf hangs down, the palm swift, unlike other birds, must incubate in an upright position by clinging to the nest with its claws. The young are born blind and naked, but have well-developed claws, for they, too, must cling to the nest during the month they remain there growing.

The common swift of Britain and Europe, which also breeds in northwest Africa and Asia, usually nests in small colonies. In towns and cities it often nests beneath the eaves of houses and in church towers and steeples. It sometimes uses old house martins' nests and nest boxes. In the past it often nested in quarries and disused woodpeckers' holes, and, in more remote places, still nests in holes in trees.

The swift frequently returns to the same nest site which it used the previous year, and as a result often pairs up with the same mate. The nest is often an untidy accumulation of material—wisps of straw and grass, feathers and even scraps of paper—which the swifts have collected on the wing. The time of laying depends to a large extent on the weather. If it is particularly wet, with the result that there are few flying insects to feed on, laying may be delayed. The normal clutch consists of two or three eggs, which are incubated by both birds and hatch after about 20 days.

The young are born helpless, blind and naked. From an early age they are capable of going for considerable lengths of time without food, a practice which is vital to their survival during periods of continuous wet weather, when food is scarce. The fledging period is rarely less than five weeks. When the young swifts leave the nest, they immediately take up an independent, airborne existence.

The swifts' closest relatives are the diminutive, jewel-like hummingbirds. Hummingbirds' nests are in most cases very delicate, elaborately made, deep, cup-shaped structures, often no bigger than half a walnut shell: the smallest nests measure just 2 cm across and 2 to 3 cm deep. Hummingbirds often build their nests on a twig or branch, or in a fork, sometimes above water. They are usually made from very fine materials such as plant fibre and down, bound together with spiders' webs. On the outside many hummingbirds place lichen, moss or tiny flakes of bark. It is often stated that this is decoration, but is more likely used to camouflage the nests. The clutch almost invariably consists of two white eggs, which take 14 days or more to hatch. The young hummingbirds are at first blind and practically naked, but grow rapidly, although they do not leave the nest until their wing feathers are fully grown. The female alone undertakes the duties of nest building, incubating the eggs and raising the young.

A similar state of affairs exists among the sunbirds, which are in many respects the Old World counterparts of the hummingbirds. Although male and female sunbirds often maintain a pair bond throughout the

Below: The rufous-breasted hummingbird fans its wings to balance itself, while feeding its young in their delicate hanging nest.

year, the nesting duties fall mainly, or in some cases entirely, to the female. The male occasionally assists with nest building and feeding the young, but the female alone incubates the eggs.

The sunbirds use similar building materials to the hummingbirds, but make very different nests. Those built by sunbirds are oval or pear-shaped and have a small opening at the side near the top; there is often a porch-like projection above the opening. A few sunbirds build neat, compact nests, but most nests have a decidedly ragged appearance. On the outside there is often lichen, moss, leaves or bark; the bottom frequently has a tail of trailing loose fibres. The nests are usually suspended from a branch fairly close to the ground. Sunbirds sometimes build close to hornets' nests and doubtless derive protection from their association with these aggressive insects, which do not harm the birds.

The nest of the long-tailed tit is often built safe within a hedge or thicket—gorse, bramble and thorn being the most popular—but is sometimes placed in a tree, often in a fork, or where a branch joins the trunk. A large ball with the entrance in the side near the top, the nest is made mainly from moss bound together with hair and spiders' webs, and on the outside is placed lichen and other materials. The inside of the nest may be lined with as many as 2,000 feathers.

It is very snug inside but hardly spacious, and the female sits with her long tail cocked up over her back while she incubates the eggs. The male may take a turn on the nest when she goes off to feed and normally he roosts in the nest above her. When after 14 to 18 days, the 7 to 12 young are hatched, both parents collect food —mainly small insects and spiders— but the male usually passes his contributions to the female, to feed to them. At about two weeks old the young long-tailed tits are almost as big as their parents.

Even more remarkable is the nest of the penduline tit, which occurs in Spain, southern France, Italy, central and Eastern Europe, and across Asia.

Above: The nest of the lesser double-collared sunbird, a native of southern Africa, is an untidy affair of grasses and leaves.

Left: A long-tailed tit visits its nest, secured between forked branches and warmly lined with downy feathers.

The penduline tit's nest is made with down from the seeds of willow and poplar, reed seed-heads, moss and grass. It is usually suspended from the end of a branch, often over or near water. The building is usually initiated by the male, who begins by twisting down and grasses around the end of the branch and, from this, weaves a hoop. Activity is next concentrated on building the base, from where the birds work upwards from the inside, and finally complete the nest by making a short entrance tube near the top. The nest takes up to two weeks to construct.

Although there is just one kind of wren living in the Old World, there are in fact 59 different species in the world. Their stronghold is in America; they occur in much of North America and throughout Central and South America.

Wrens usually build large bulky nests, with the entrance in the side. Many nests are solely the work of the male wren. The males of many species, several of which are known or believed to be to some extent polygamous (meaning that they take more than one mate), have a strong urge to build nests. Males sometimes build as many as six. The female wren usually chooses the best nest, which she titivates and lines with soft materials. The nests which she rejects are often flimsy and poorly, if at all, concealed. These are known as 'cocks' nests' and the males often sleep in them. These nests also help distract attention from the nest in which the female is incubating the eggs. Although incubation is solely the duty of the female wren, the male sometimes feeds her at the nest and helps rear the young.

Among the most ingenious of all builders are the aptly-named tailorbirds, which live in South-East Asia. They are small birds with fairly long, straight beaks and tails, which they hold erect, rather in the manner of wrens. Tailorbirds select a single large leaf or two or more smaller leaves. Then they push silk threads, kapok, odd pieces of wool or strands of cotton through small holes made with their sharp beaks, along the edges of the leaf or leaves. They work their way around, loosely drawing or 'stitching' together the edges, until eventually a pocket is formed.

Most of the work is done by the females. The males concentrate on patrolling their territories, calling loudly as they go, although they do give more practical assistance during the later stages of building by bringing some of the materials. In the pocket the tailorbirds build their nest, which with help from the males is usually completed in about four days. The nest fits snugly into the pocket.

Some of the most curious and unlikely nest places are chosen by the robin. Besides its more usual nest sites in banks, under tussocks, among roots and stumps, and in holes in trees and walls, the robin commonly nests in old pots and pans, in sheds, in vehicles and even in the pockets of coats hung behind doors.

The rather bulky open nest is made mainly from dead leaves and moss, and lined with fine rootlets, hairs and feathers. Five to seven white or bluish-white eggs, speckled with pale red, are laid, which hatch after 12 to 14 days. Both parents rear the young and as three broods during a summer are not uncommon, they have a busy time. The male often looks after the earlier brood while his mate is laying and hatching the next. The young robins fly after about 15 days.

Curious hanging, pouch-like nests are woven by the oropendolas and caciques, larger American relatives of the colourful American orioles. They live in tropical Central and South America, and some of them breed during the summer in the USA and Canada. The oropendolas are gregarious birds that nest in colonies, usually in a tall isolated tree in a clearing, or one which towers above the surrounding trees. The nests,

Below: A robin at its nest. The bright gape of the nestlings' beaks stimulates the parent birds to supply them with food.

which often number from 12 to 40 in a colony, are suspended from the ends of horizontal branches. The oropendolas' woven nesting pouches, some of them a metre long or more, have the entrance at the top, with the nest itself, which is often lined with dead leaves, at the bottom. The females alone do the building. They also incubate the eggs, which take about 14 days to hatch, and care for the young during the month or more they are in the nests. The males are polygamous (they mate with more than one female) and take virtually no part in the nesting proceedings, but move about the tree tops and act as guardians or watchmen.

The caciques, too, are gregarious, and roost together and nest in colonies. A colony of the yellow-rumped cacique, a pale-blue-eyed, otherwise mostly black coloured bird, often contains as many as 40 to 50 nests, touching each other in thick clusters at the ends of branches. The nests are built by the females from plant fibres, and are yellowish in colour. Members of the colony do not all begin nesting at the same time, with the result that there are often some nests under construction, others containing fresh eggs, or partly incubated eggs, as well as young at all stages of development.

In practically every yellow-rumped cacique colony are a pair of piratic flycatchers, which lay their eggs and raise their young in a cacique's nest which they take over. The giant cowbird, which is parasitic in a similar manner to the cuckoo, lays its eggs in the nests of caciques and oropendolas, leaving them to hatch the eggs and raise the young cowbirds with their own.

In tropical Africa and South-East Asia, many trees are festooned with what may appear to be strange, exotic fruits, but are, in fact, the nests made by weaver birds. Whereas most other species of small birds go to considerable lengths to conceal their nests, weaver birds make little or no attempt to hide theirs. In fact, the reverse seems to be true: frequently they live in large colonies, and almost cover trees, bushes and other vegetation such as reed-beds with their close-slung nests.

Their nests, usually globe-shaped, are often finely woven from grasses, palm leaves or other pliable plant material. Access to the nests is usually by an entrance tube, sometimes as long as 60 cm, which hangs from the underside and acts as an anti-predator device. Doubtless for the same reason, the nests are usually suspended from the ends of branches or palm leaves, often over water. Several kinds of weaver live and nest in and around villages and towns and even in cities, a good example being the village or black-headed weaver.

Weaver bird colonies are usually very noisy; the occupants chatter and bicker incessantly, and there is a constant coming and going of birds. Most weavers are about the size of a sparrow or a little smaller. With the coming of the breeding season, most males assume bright, mainly yellow and black, or red or orange and black, plumage. By comparison the females are rather dull, sparrow-like birds. The males of these species are usually polygamous. The males often build several nests, advertising each to the females by hanging upside down from the entrance, fluttering their wings and chattering loudly.

Left: Like ornaments on a Christmas tree, the nests of a colony of spotted-backed weavers festoon a palm tree.

Several kinds of weaver are regarded as serious pests, by far the worst of these being the sparrow-like red-billed quelea. This quelea is extremely gregarious and occurs in enormous flocks which often number more than a million birds. Flocks gather in tremendous numbers where rice or grain is grown. A flock of a million red-billed queleas can destroy as much as 60 tonnes of grain in one day.

The queleas build their nests close together, sometimes so much so that the nest backs become woven together. The males build the nests ready for the arrival of the females, taking only a few days to do so. Small trees often hold about 500 nests each, and larger trees up to 6,000 nests. It is estimated that some sites contain ten million or more nests.

The social weaver, which lives in dry, inhospitable parts of south-west Africa, builds the most incredible communal tenement. Perhaps the work of three hundred or more birds, this 'super nest' may measure 9 × 6 m at the base and be 1.5 m or more high. Usually built in a camel-thorn or other large tree standing alone, it even boasts a roof which all the members of the colony, male and female, build and maintain. It is so expertly thatched with grasses that during the sporadic heavy rains, the water simply drains off. Beneath the protection of the roof the birds build their own nests. There may be a hundred or more individual nests united under a single roof.

Each nest has an entrance tunnel which leads to the nesting chamber in which the weavers lay their three or four eggs. When the chamber is not being used for nesting, the birds sleep in it. The rosy or peach-faced lovebird, scaly-crowned weaver and red-headed finch are among several kinds of birds which sometimes take up residence in empty nests or may eject the rightful owners. However, they never take over the entire structure and all the birds live together beneath the same roof. Another bird which sometimes moves in is the smallest African bird of prey, the pygmy falcon. The weavers do not object to the presence of the tiny falcon, which does not molest its hosts.

Snakes such as the Cape cobra and boomslang have little difficulty raiding the nest chambers, and take a heavy toll of eggs and young birds. The ratel or honey badger sometimes manages to climb the nesting tree and uses its strong claws to break open the nests and eats any young it can find.

The social weaver's massive tenement often grows bigger each season as more birds join the colony, and is commonly used for up to 20 years.

Left: The nest of a Hartlaub's weaver is as intricate, if not quite as tidy, as those of most other weaver birds.

Below: A little weaver, in breeding plumage, at its suspended nest. The male weaver birds usually construct the nests and then try to attract the females to occupy them.

A structure similar to the social weaver's is built by the South American quaker parakeet: a building feat unique among members of the parrot family. Built in the uppermost branches of a tree, it is made from thorny twigs, presumably because they bind together well and provide good protection against predators. Each pair of parakeets have their own nest within the main structure, which is formed over a number of years as birds build their nests alongside and on top of existing nests. Up to 20 nests have been recorded in one structure, although less than half this number is more usual.

The quaker parakeet's home is used throughout the year as roosting quarters. With the approach of the breeding season the parakeets begin to add material and repair any damage. The breeding season commences in October and the usual clutch consists of five to six white eggs, which are incubated by the female.

Despite the structure's untidy, loose appearance, it is remarkably strong. This strength is well demonstrated by the fact that large birds such as the jabiru stork, birds of prey and whistling ducks sometimes nest on the top.

Among the largest individual nests are those built by birds of prey. Some species that nest in trees prefer to use the old nests of other birds. But many, including the eagles, build their own nests, which are used year after year. (A nest of a crowned hawk eagle in South Africa is said to have been in regular use for more than 70 years.) More material is added to the nests each year and they often reach an enormous size. One golden eagle's nest, or eyrie, in a pine tree was 1.5 m across and 5 m deep: such a nest may contain more than a tonne of sticks and other material. Nests sometimes become so heavy that eventually they collapse during a gale or storm, or because the tree is unable to withstand the weight and the branches break or the tree topples over.

The nest of the osprey is also used year after year and may measure 1 m across and as much as 2 m deep. It is made mainly from branches and sticks. Both the male and female osprey build and repair the nest. The female arranges most of the material, the majority of which is brought by the male. The inside of the nest is lined with grass and other soft materials, and is added to throughout the breeding season.

Like those made by the eagles and the ospreys, the nests built by the storks are often sizeable structures. Most storks nest in trees, although some, such as the black stork, may build on rocky ledges. The white stork has come to prefer nesting on buildings such as churches, ruins, chimneys, telegraph poles and special nesting platforms put up to encourage these well-loved birds. This stork's nest often measures 2 m across. It is basically a platform of sticks and twigs to which may be added rags, paper and other rubbish. After a bad winter the storks sometimes return to find that their nests need to be completely rebuilt, although normally this it is not necessary and more material is simply added each year.

Below: A pair of ospreys and their young in their huge nest, set beside the water from which the adult birds snatch fish prey to feed the family.

Smaller birds, including sparrows, often build their own nests in the base of the stork's nest, as they do in the nests of the osprey and some other birds of prey. Often this is simply a case of using an available, if somewhat unusual, nesting site, but sometimes (as with those sunbirds which build close to hornets' nests) the smaller birds derive some protection from their association with the bigger birds.

Some birds of prey make use of nests made by other birds, particularly members of the crow family. These tend to be bulky structures made mainly from sticks and twigs. The nests built by magpies are usually enclosed. The main body of the magpie's nest is made from sticks, very often thorny or prickly ones, and is lined with mud, then a softer lining of fine rootlets, grasses and similar materials. The nest, which is built by both the male and female, has a small and inconspicuous side entrance. Old nests are sometimes taken over by a pair of kestrels, which also use other crows' nests.

The rook nests in large colonies, usually high in the tree tops. These colonies are known as rookeries, a term which is also commonly used to describe colonies of some other kinds of birds, including penguins, and sometimes even mammals such as seals. Some members of the crow family, such as tropical jays, lay only two to four eggs, but other crows lay up to nine eggs. The colours range from cream and buff to green and greenish-blue, heavily blotched or spotted with brown or other colours. Incubation takes from 16–21 days and the young are hatched blind, helpless and naked, or nearly so.

Closely related to the crows are the birds of paradise and the bowerbirds. The male birds of paradise are renowned for their brilliantly coloured and often bizarre plumage, and for the dances and other spectacular displays which many perform in order to attract the attention of the females. Some male bowerbirds are brightly coloured and a few have crests or other head decorations, but none possess the incredible gaudy plumage of some of the male birds of paradise. However, as if to compensate, most have developed quite exceptional skills as builders and decorators. The males use their skills not for nest construction, but to build 'bowers' which they decorate, and in some cases even 'paint', with the aim of attracting a female. The bowers have no direct connection with the birds' nests, which are always built by the females in trees, usually some distance away.

The best known of the bowerbirds are the so-called avenue builders. These are widespread in Australia and New Guinea. One, the jackdaw-sized satin bowerbird, is native to eastern Australia. The male satin bowerbird places upright into a bed of twigs on the ground thousands of small twigs in two tight-knit parallel rows to form an avenue or bower. This is always aligned in a north-to-south direction. The male satin bowerbird decorates the bower with a variety of extra-

Above: The white stork—this one is nesting in the ruins of the Roman city of Volubilis in North Africa—has become the symbol of parenthood. Like many migratory birds it returns annually to the same breeding location.

ordinary paraphernalia, particularly blue objects, including feathers shed by rosella parakeets and discarded rubbish like blue cigarette packets and matchboxes, bottle tops and other junk. It is thought that the male satin bowerbird probably prefers blue objects because of their resemblance to the colour of rival males. There are sometimes also a few greenish or grey objects, colours like those of the female. The bower is jealously guarded and the male often has to drive off neighbouring rivals that attempt to steal his objects.

During the height of the breeding season, which is in spring and early summer, the male satin bowerbird also paints his bower almost daily. He paints it with chewed-up fruit pulp or charcoal, using a wad of leaves or a piece of bark as a 'paint brush'. This usually does the trick and eventually he succeeds in attracting a female to his bower. This makes him very excited and he dances and shows off to her. He often displays to her with one of the blue objects from the bower held in his beak.

The displays sometimes continue for a considerable length of time, until there is an abundance of the insects on which the young will be fed. It is only then that the female mates with the male. She then goes off on her own to build a shallow nest of twigs, some distance from the ground in a forest tree. She incubates the one to three eggs and raises the young.

Some of the other bowerbirds—the maypole builders—erect such remarkable large edifices that it is difficult to believe that they are the work of quite small birds. The male golden or Newton's bowerbird of northern Queensland, Australia, although only about 24 cm long, constructs a maypole or bower some 2.3 m high, or even as high as 3 m, according to some authorities. The male usually makes two cones by piling twigs around the bases of two nearby saplings, joined at 30 cm or higher above the ground by a horizontal 'display' branch or bridge. The twigs are stuck together with a sticky fungus, which is common in the forest. He collects lichens and usually either green or white flowers, which he places in gaps between the twigs at the base of the cones and at the ends of the display perch.

The similarly-sized, drab-coloured male gardener bowerbird of New Guinea builds an extraordinary structure like a miniature, conical, thatched hut, about a metre high, around one or more saplings. True to its name the gardener bowerbird sets out before it a carefully tended garden, decorated with fruit, flowers, beetles' wing-cases and other colourful objects.

Australia and New Guinea are also a stronghold of another group of remarkable birds, the megapodes. Whereas all the previous birds incubate their eggs using their own body heat, the megapodes (known by a variety of common names) lay their eggs in holes dug in the ground, or build their own incubators from mounds of rotting vegetation, and hatch their eggs in these.

One of the megapodes, the Australian brush turkey, builds a mound about 2.5 to 4 m in diameter and 1 m

Above: A male Australian satin bowerbird surveys the progress of his work as he builds and decorates his bower, ready to impress his would-be wife.

high, made mainly from leaves and twigs raked up from the forest floor. In the warm, humid forest the mound ferments rapidly and generates considerable heat, and is carefully tended by the male bird so that the correct temperature is maintained to hatch the eggs.

The mallee fowl is almost exclusively an inhabitant of the dry scrubland of south-western Australia. It is the only megapode which lives in such a dry habitat. The mallee fowl dig a hole about 60 cm deep in the sandy soil, or clears out an old mound. Twigs and leaves are gathered from the surrounding area and heaped into the hole. By August, when all of the accumulated material has been thoroughly dampened by rain, the birds begin to prepare the egg chamber. A hole is dug in the centre, from which all large sticks are removed, and this is filled with a mixture of leaves and sandy soil. As a result of the excavations there is eventually a mound almost 5 m in diameter and 1 m high, with the egg chamber in the centre.

The female lays from 5 to 35 eggs, although 15 to 24 is a more usual number. The eggs are laid at intervals of about one week, and each takes about eight weeks to hatch. Cut off from the dry air, the matter in the mound ferments and generates heat, which is supplemented by heat from the sun. Throughout incubation, which extends from September to March or April, the male tends the mound. He keeps the temperature of the chamber within one degree of 33 °C, either by adding or scraping away some of the insulating layer of soil, a fantastic piece of thermal engineering.

As the eggs are laid over a period of several months, the earlier eggs hatch and the chicks depart before the final eggs are laid. The chicks take several hours to dig their way out of the mound. They do it without any help from their parents.

Below: The male regent bowerbird, like other bowerbirds, is brightly coloured, while the female is a drab creature.

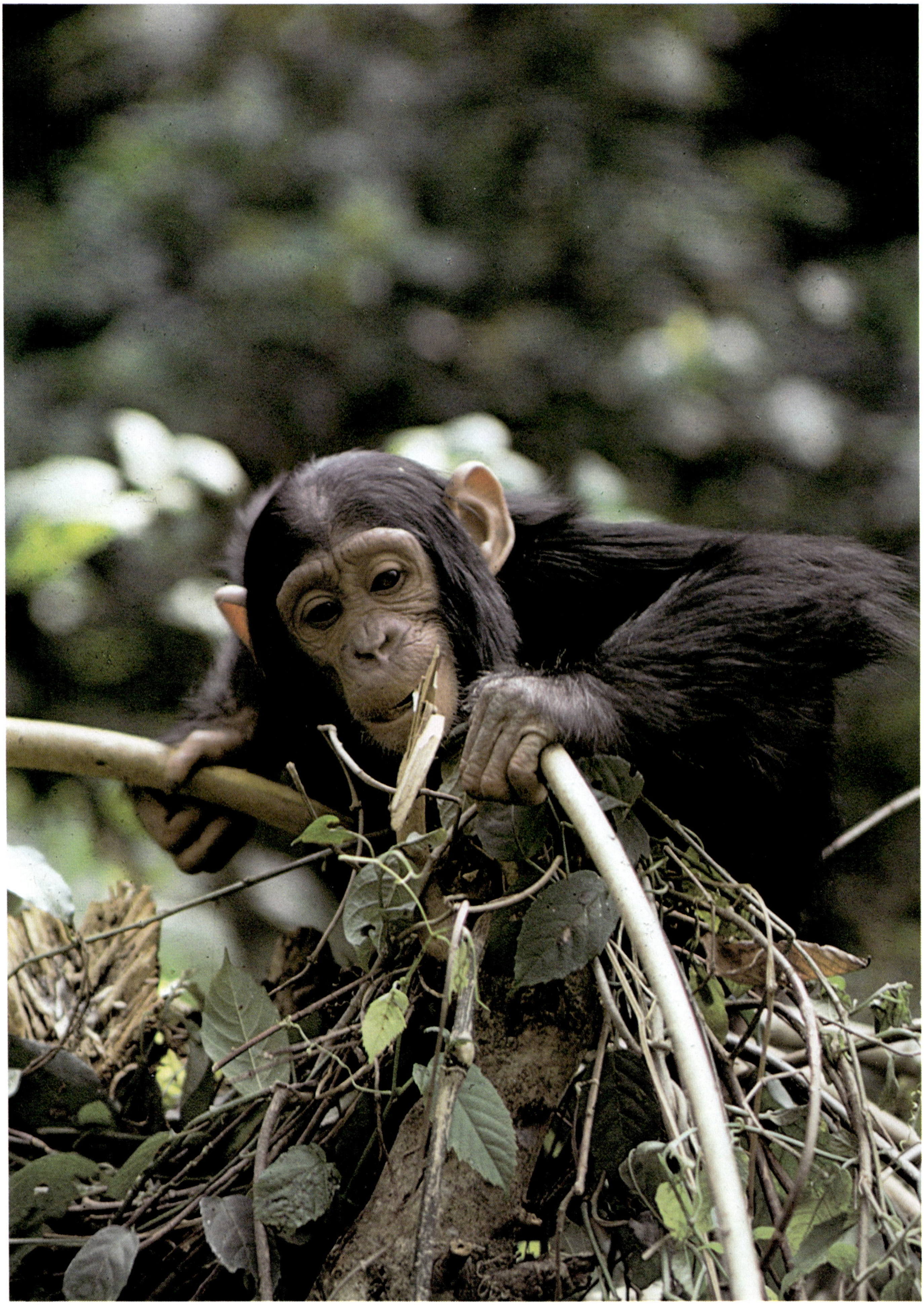

Mammals as Builders

Apart from humans, there are surprisingly few mammal builders. Even the great apes—our nearest relatives—only erect rudimentary sleeping platforms of leaves and branches, which are generally built afresh every night. Why mammals do not build more is difficult to say. Indeed, the exquisite little structures built by the harvest mouse prove that some mammals certainly have it in them to build proficiently.

Of the few mammals which do habitually construct homes, the beaver of Europe, Asia and North America is by far the most dedicated. Not only does it build an elaborate home, called a lodge, but it also indulges in great hydro-engineering feats in order to create an aquatic environment exactly to its liking.

On wide, free-flowing rivers where the water level remains fairly constant, the beaver is content to dig a chamber into the bank, piling sticks on top if the water does rise. But in a shallow, sluggish river, or in a pond made by the beaver's own dams, the beaver builds its lodge surrounded by water. Saturated sticks are piled up on the river bed to a height of 2 to 3 m above the water. Inside this woodpile the beaver fashions its living chamber.

Upstream and downstream of the lodge are the dams, and it is these which are really astonishing. A skilled hydro-engineer cannot maintain a water level better than a team of beavers working together. Dams often reach 80 to 100 m long, and the longest ever recorded is no less than 700 m, on the Jefferson River in Montana, USA, which can easily bear the weight of a man on horseback. Other great beaver structures are located in the Mississippi swamps.

The dams are expertly built on a foundation of strong sticks, which are rammed into the river bed with considerable force and anchored to a nearby tree. Smaller sticks are interlaced, and the whole dam is weighed down with logs and rocks and supported against the current by forked poles wedged against boulders. Any gaps are plugged with mud and reeds until the structure is completely watertight and dry.

The beaver is as efficient at cutting and transporting its raw material as it is at constructing it. Trees are felled and logs and branches cut to length by the beaver's immensely strong and sharp chisel-shaped incisor teeth. Tree trunks standing away from the waterside are transported to the river along a series of cleared lanes, or specially built canals.

The actual building work is done literally by hand; stones and brushwood are also collected in this way. Breaches in the dams are rapidly found and repaired, and changes in the water level equally quickly compensated for by work at one or both of the dams. Even more remarkably, during severe weather, when their ponds are covered by a layer of thick ice, the beavers adjust the downstream dam to lower the water level so that there is a breathing space between the ice and the water.

Not surprisingly, the beaver has an exceptionally well-developed brain for a rodent, and because of its many skills and abilities it is perhaps the most accomplished of all animal builders.

The only other animal to construct anything like the beaver's dams is the muskrat or musquash—another large rodent of North America. It builds

Opposite: Breaking off branches and twisting them into a rough platform, a chimpanzee sets about making his bed for the night.

Left: Perhaps the most accomplished of animal builders, the beaver constructs dams which can divert rivers and alter the geography of the landscape.

Top: A muskrat puts the final touches to the large heap of vegetation that contains its living quarters, entered from below water level.

Bottom: In the foreground water surges against a beaver dam, while behind, its huge nest-pile or lodge rises like an island out of the beaver's private 'swimming pool'.

houses out of large mounds of vegetation, 1 m or more high, on riverbanks —as the beaver sometimes does—and constructs canal systems wherever the country is suitably flat, for example, in marshes. The muskrat, however, does not build lodges surrounded by water, and certainly cannot construct the beaver's elaborate dams.

But when it comes to the home, the muskrat's style resembles the beaver's quite closely: where the river has a high bank, the muskrat is content to excavate its living chamber, but where this is not possible it runs its tunnel up and into a pile of sticks. The entrances are always below water level so that, like the beaver, the muskrat can come and go unwitnessed.

Top: The desert wood rat, foraging under a cactus, uses the spines of these plants to protect its nest.

Middle: The bushy-tailed wood rat. Wood rats are also known as pack or trade rats, because of their habit of stealing small objects to decorate their nests, and replacing the objects with pebbles.

Bottom: A young red squirrel grooms itself in its native pine trees. The nests or 'dreys' of squirrels are often converted from crows' nests.

The muskrat stores food for the winter in its home; the beaver, however, usually anchors its winter fodder with stones at the bottom of the river near its front entrance.

A group of 20 western North American rodents called wood rats also show considerable cleverness in building their homes. One, the dusky-footed rat, builds a structure more than 1 m high. It may contain as many as five inter-connecting chambers: a living chamber, nursery, storage chambers and lavatory. Not content with that, it often builds an equally elaborate second home close by in the branches of a tree, probably as a retreat when danger threatens at ground level. Another species of rat builds its home amongst cacti, and places spiky pieces in all the entrances to deter undesirable callers. The rat itself seems to be able to move among the sharp spines with impunity.

The bushy-tailed pack rat decorates its lodge with brightly-coloured objects, in much the same way as the bowerbird, except that the lodge is not thought to be for courtship.

Squirrels are among the best-known mammal builders. Their large 'dreys' or nests are well-known to people living near wooded country; but in the leafless winter, trees betray their occupants to forestry workers, to whom squirrels—especially the grey squirrel —are a serious nuisance. The red squirrel, which occurs across Europe to Asia and Japan, is Britain's native squirrel, but the North American grey squirrel has quickly established itself, and is now by far the commonest kind in Britain; the red squirrel is now restricted to just a few remaining strongholds, especially in pine forests.

Both species build round homes high up in trees where a stout branch joins the trunk, so that they are subject to the least buffeting by the wind. Dreys are constructed of thick branches and bark, and form a rough but remarkably strong structure. Sometimes an old crow's nest is used as a foundation: the walls are built up into a domed roof with sturdy sticks, usually from the same tree.

Once the main structure is com-

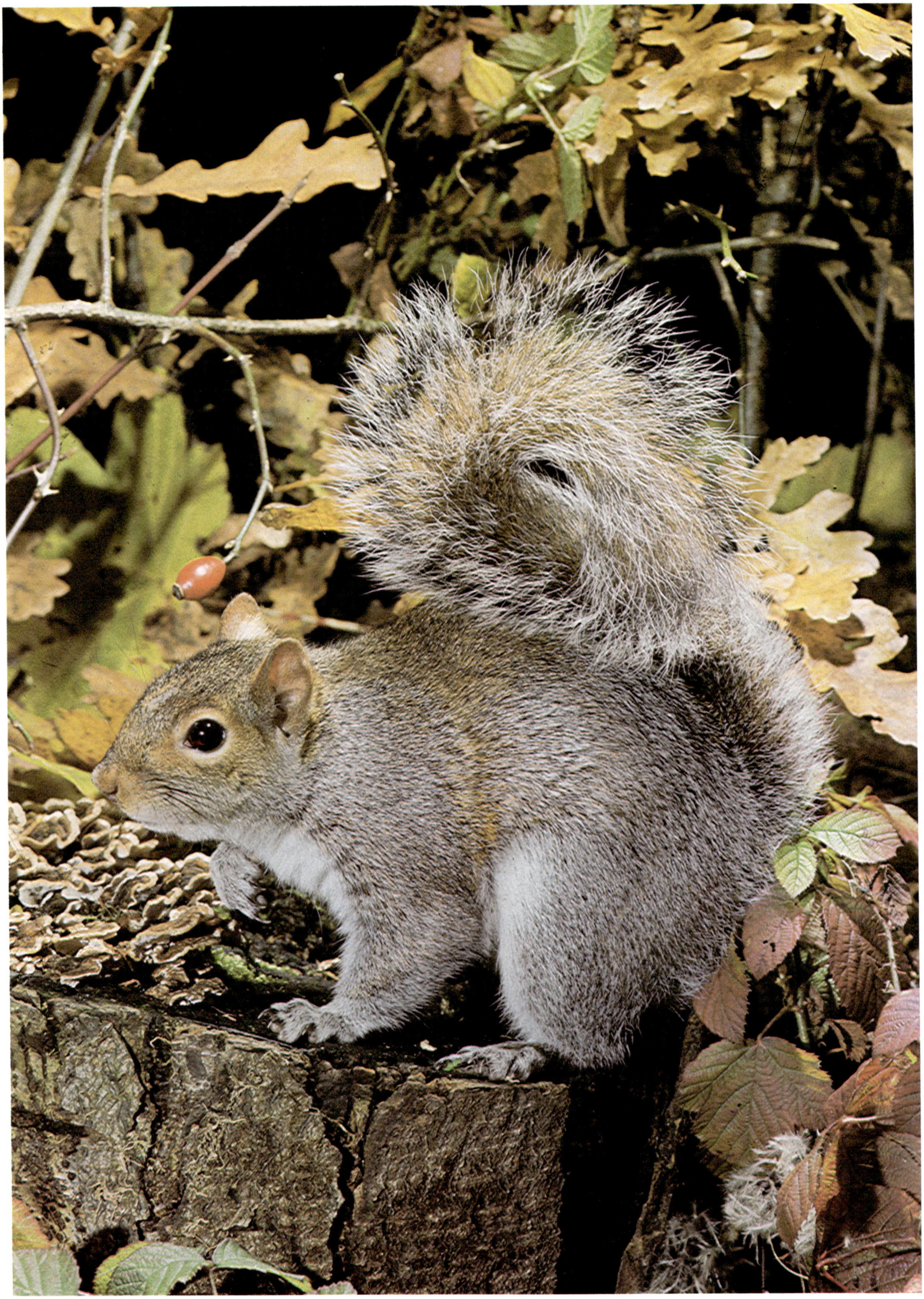

plete, all holes and gaps are stopped up with thinner, more pliable sticks which are wedged into place by the squirrel's paws and teeth. Lining the interior of the drey are much softer materials such as grass, roots and bark fibre, and forming the floor is a cushion of finely-shredded grass, leaves, moss and so on.

Apart from their main home—where the young are reared—some squirrels build secondary refuges, and in summer the grey squirrel, in particular, will also build platforms on the ends of branches. In the breeding season, squirrels often camouflage the drey with twigs and branches still bearing green leaves or pine needles.

While the squirrels build in European trees, the apes build in the African jungle. The sleeping platforms of the great apes are not in themselves particularly inspiring. But on two counts at least, they demand examination. As far as we know these are almost the only structures actually built by any of the primates, which, having opposable thumbs, are the animals best equipped to perform manipulatory tasks. Secondly, despite their apparent coarseness, the nests are deceptively well-made by the animals, in a very short time.

Most chimpanzees build a new nest in the forest each night. After a suitably firm site has been found in the crown of a tree, the chimpanzee bends the branches inwards and intertwines them so that they remain firm. Smaller leafy twigs are then added to form a cushioned bed surface. Quite often the chimpanzee places another handful or two of leafy twigs under its head or some other part of the body as a pillow.

The construction only takes about

Opposite: The grey squirrel builds nests both for its own shelter and to house its litters of young.

Left: In the forest canopy of equatorial Africa, a young chimpanzee makes quite a mess of learning how to construct its sleeping platform.

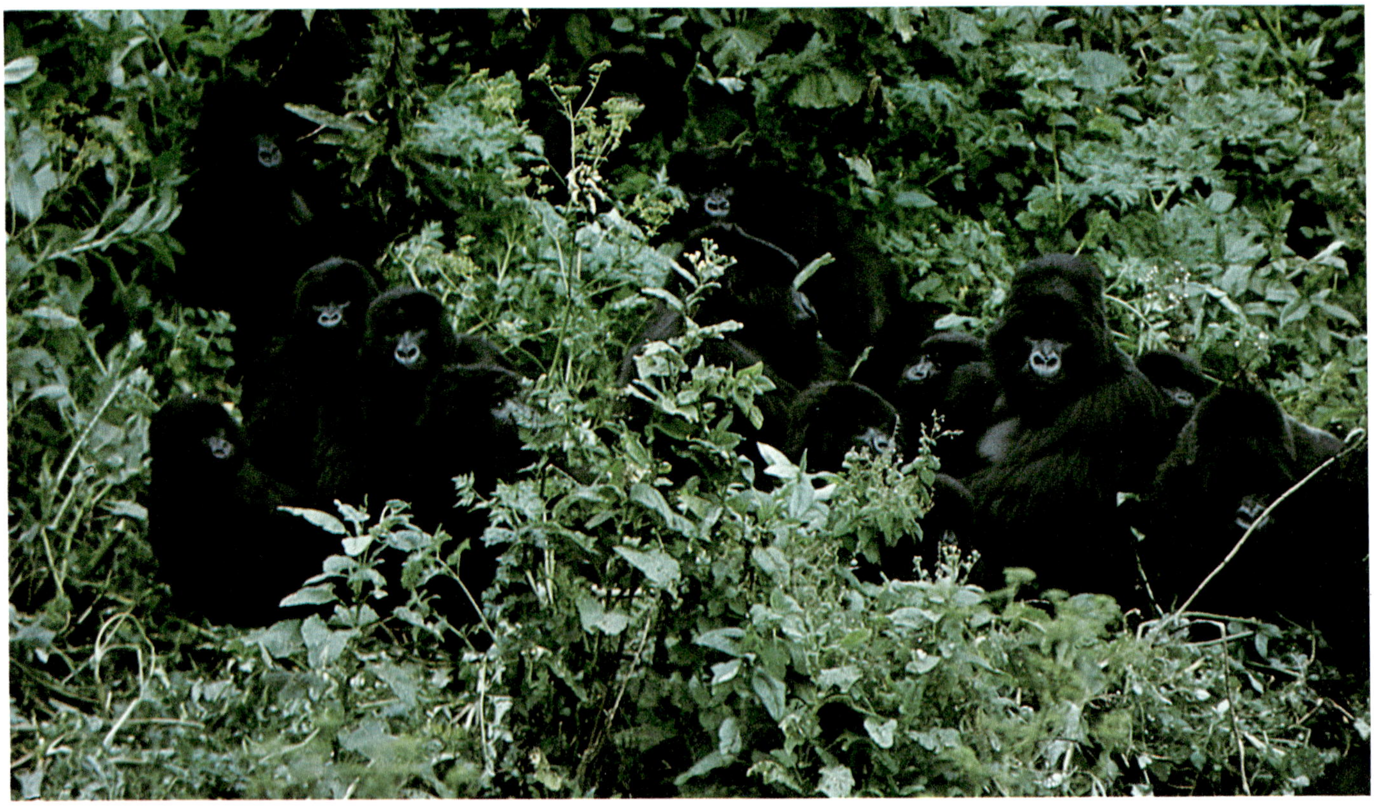

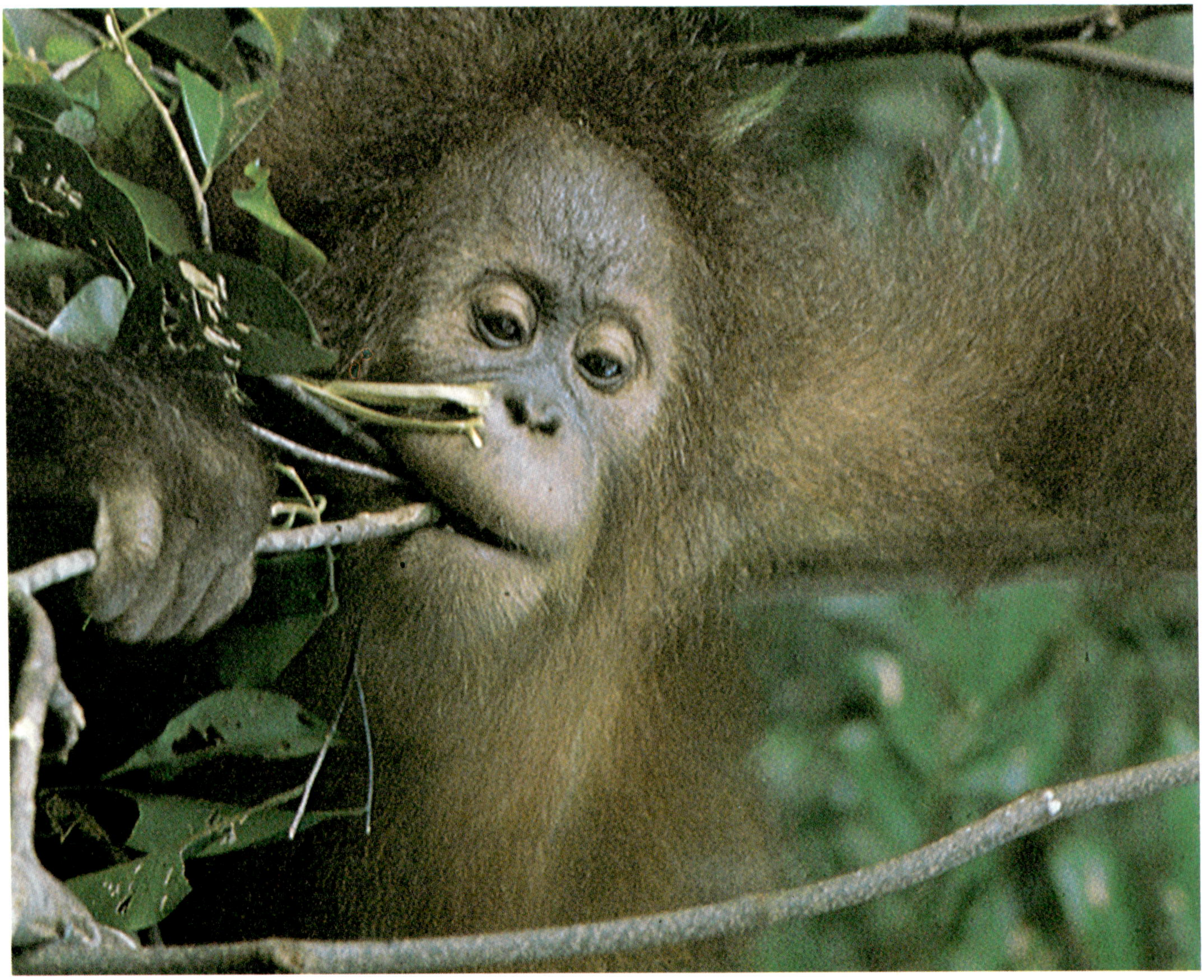

four minutes, but a mother holding an infant with one hand takes about twice as long, partly because of her burden and partly because she makes a larger nest. During the four years while young chimpanzees are dependent on their mothers, they experiment a lot and soon learn to build their own nests, even though they do not need to do so in earnest for some time.

The orang-utan of South-East Asia builds very similar platforms to those of the chimpanzee. The gorilla, which also lives in Africa, behaves similarly, although it spends more time on the ground and often makes its bed there. Gorillas tend to use the same nest for as long as the family remains in one area.

Not very long ago the aye-aye was thought to be extinct. In fact just a few individuals in the Malagasy Republic (Madagascar) grimly hang on to survival. It is one of the most primitive and specialized of all the primates, and has no close relatives.

One of the ways in which the aye-aye differs from its more modern monkey cousins is in being something of a builder. In the remote bamboo forests of north-western Madagascar the aye-aye builds a spherical nest with a side entrance, either in a hollow tree or on a branch against the tree. It is a breeding nest measuring about 50 cm in diameter in which the mother gives birth to a single baby in February or March. Very little is known about the family life of this rare and most interesting animal.

In the spring, the common dormouse builds itself a summer sleeping nest off the ground in tangled vegetation. This nest is constructed of grasses and lined with moss and leaves. The female's breeding nest is larger, better

Opposite, top: The mountain gorillas have good reason to be shy, since hunters have brought them to the edge of extinction.

Opposite, bottom: An orang-utan, or 'old man of the forest', uses his teeth to break up twigs to line his sleeping platform.

Left: Confined to a few areas of bamboo forest in the Malagasy Republic, the rare aye-aye is known to build a nest in which it raises its infant.

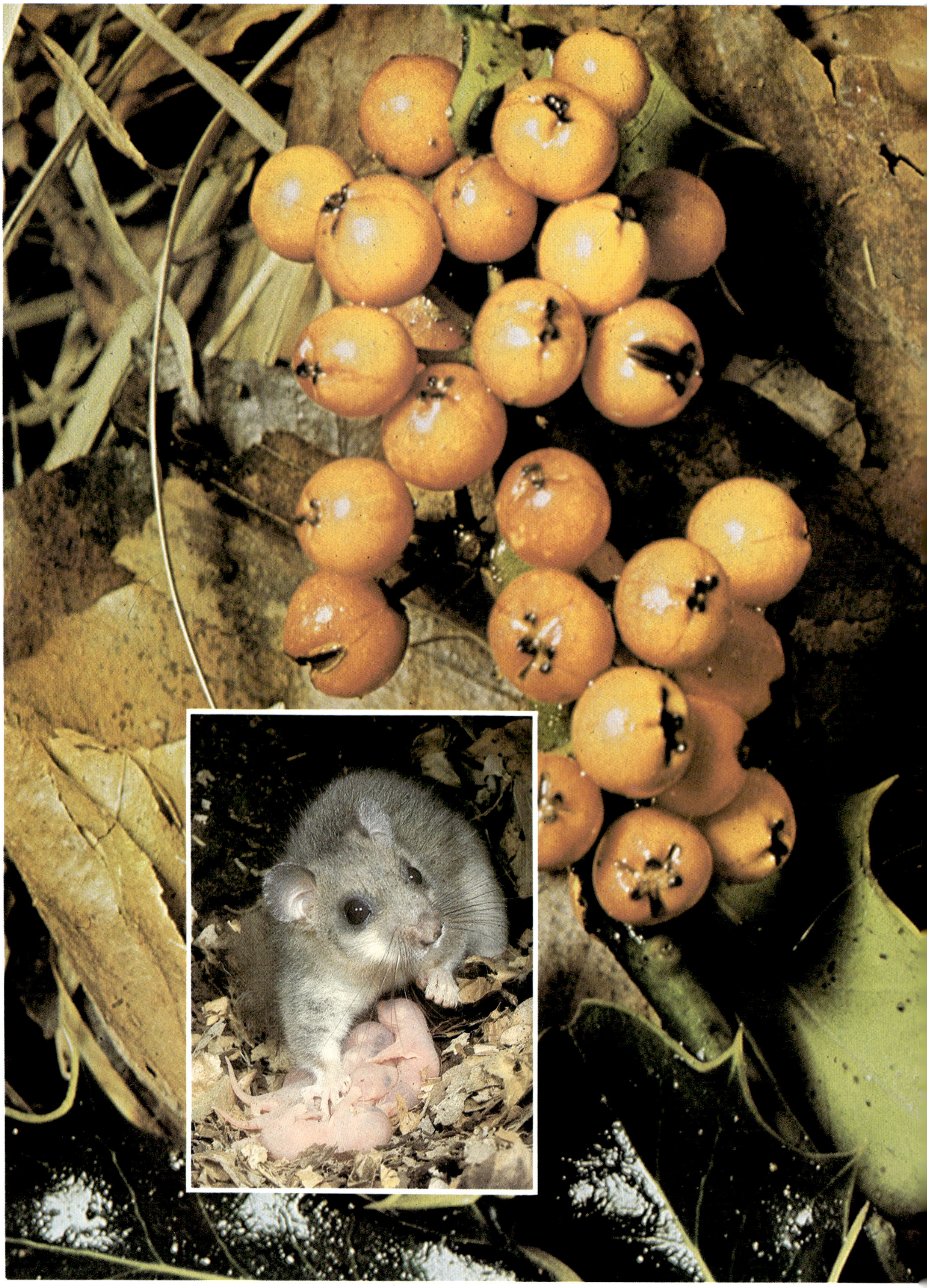

Left: The dormouse, like many other small rodents, is a prolific builder, making both sleeping nests and more elaborate nests to rear its young (inset). When ready to hibernate, after fattening up on nuts (see top of picture), it rolls up in a warm mound of dry leaves.

built and usually nearer the ground than the sleeping nests.

When it is ready to hibernate the dormouse constructs a similar nest but places it in deep litter or beneath good cover. The fat it has put on in the autumn feeds the sleeping animal, but sometimes it wakes up and has a snack from its store of nuts and seeds which it collected the preceding autumn.

The most intricate and bird-like of all nests built by mammals are the exquisite little round balls woven by the harvest mouse—a very small rodent measuring only about 6 cm long, not including the tail.

The harvest mouse lives in grain fields (mostly wheat and oats), meadows, or wherever there are suitably strong, grassy stems to support its main home about 46 cm above ground level. Less carefully built sleeping nests are also erected by young and old alike.

Winter nests, a little larger, are built in autumn in a bank or some other sheltered place, and well stocked with provisions. Some particularly intelligent individuals will even winter in granaries and barns, where there is a constant supply of food.

The harvest mouse is an industrious, agile animal which clambers nimbly about the vegetation using its prehensile tail as an extra limb. Early in the season nests are often made in hedgerows, but later on when the wheat stalks have grown up, these are preferred for nest building. When all the stalks growing within reach of the new nest have been used, the harvest mouse collects more and shreds them lengthways with its sharp incisor teeth. The nest is reinforced until it is very strong, and lined with warm, soft materials.

The female harvest mouse has to build several new nests a year—one for each litter of 3 to 6 young. Despite the workmanship involved, each nest only takes 5 to 10 hours to build.

The lemming, best known for its apparently suicidal migration, is also one of the few mammals to build a structure above the ground; although, more often than not, the neat little round nest of shredded roots, moss and lichen is located under the cover of a rock or even within a burrow. Several litters of 3 to 9 young are produced each year.

During the harsh winters experienced in its northern homelands, the Norwegian lemming burrows extensively in the snow. When spring comes and the snow melts, the winter nest can sometimes be seen suspended in mid-air, attached to a growing twig.

Opposite: The tiny nests of harvest mice are woven from the stems and leaves of grain crops such as wheat, so that the nest is suspended close to the animals' food supply.

Below: Harvest mice have been known to occupy the abandoned nests of other creatures, like this mouse which is using a wren's nest.